Rockabilly Ladies with The Ugly Duckling Fairy Tale Coloring Book Book

THE UGLY DUCKLING

IT was so beautiful in the country. It was the summer time. The wheat fields were golden, the oats were green, and the hay stood in great stacks in the green meadows. The stork paraded about among them on his long red legs, chattering away in Egyptian, the language he had learned from his lady mother.

All around the meadows and cornfields grew thick woods, and in the midst of the forest was a deep lake. Yes, it was beautiful, it was delightful in the country.

In a sunny spot stood a pleasant old farmhouse circled all about with deep canals; and from the walls down to the water's edge grew great burdocks, so high that under the tallest of them a little child might stand upright. The spot was as wild as if it had been in the very center of the thick wood.

In this snug retreat sat a duck upon her nest, watching for her young brood to hatch; but the pleasure she had felt at first was almost gone; she had begun to think it a wearisome task, for the little ones were so long coming out of their shells, and she seldom had visitors. The other ducks liked much better to swim about in the canals than to climb the slippery banks and sit under the burdock leaves to have a gossip with her. It was a long time to stay so much by herself.

At length, however, one shell cracked, and soon another, and from each came a living creature that lifted its head and cried "Peep, peep."

"Quack, quack!" said the mother; and then they all tried to say it, too, as well as they could, while they looked all about them on every side at the tall green leaves. Their mother allowed them to look about as much as they liked, because green is good for the eyes.

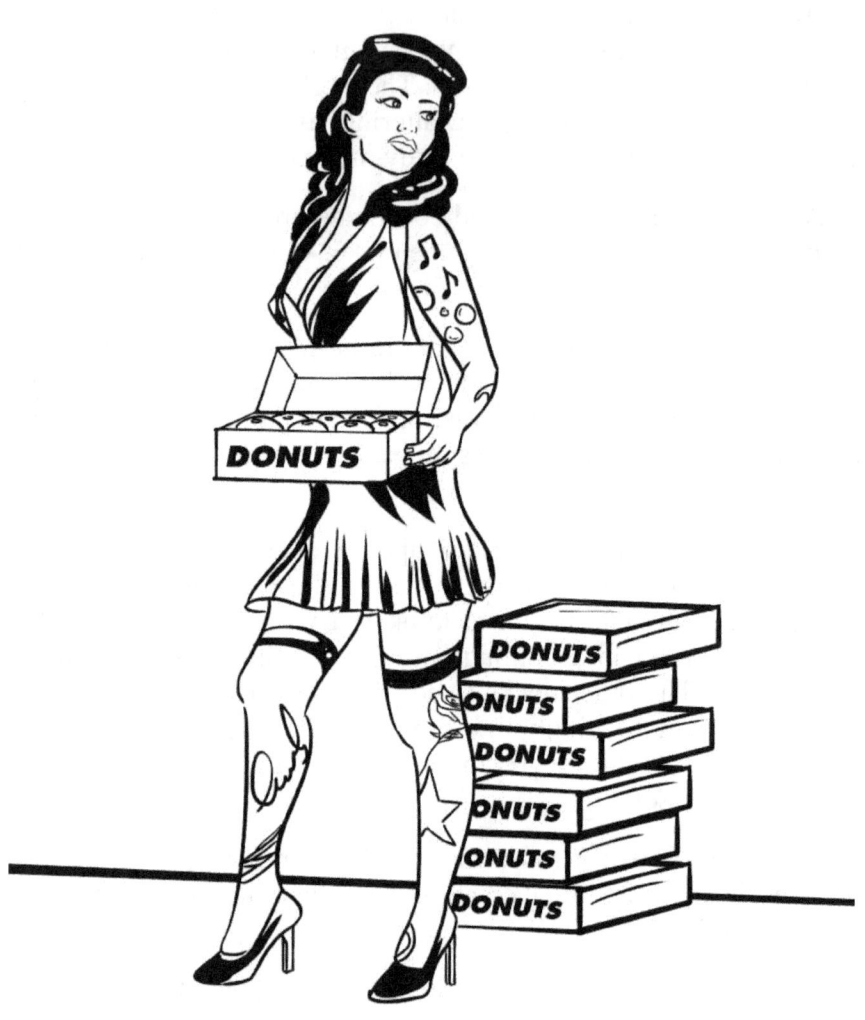

Chicken Scratch

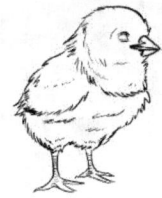

"What a great world it is, to be sure," said the little ones, when they found how much more room they had than when they were in the eggshell.

"Is this all the world, do you imagine?" said the mother. "Wait till you have seen the garden. Far beyond that it stretches down to the pastor's field, though I have never ventured to such a distance. Are you all out?" she continued, rising to look. "No, not all; the largest egg lies there yet, I declare. I wonder how long this business is to last. I'm really beginning to be tired of it;" but for all that she sat down again.

"Well, and how are you to-day?" quacked an old duck who came to pay her a visit.

"There's one egg that takes a deal of hatching. The shell is hard and will not break," said the fond mother, who sat still upon her nest. "But just look at the others. Have I not a pretty family? Are they not the prettiest little ducklings you ever saw? They are the image of their father—the good for naught! He never comes to see me."

"Let me see the egg that will not break," said the old duck. "I've no doubt it's a Guinea fowl's egg. The same thing happened to me once, and a deal of trouble it gave me, for the young ones are afraid of the water. I quacked[33] and clucked, but all to no purpose. Let me take a look at it. Yes, I am right; it's a Guinea fowl, upon my word; so take my advice and leave it where it is. Come to the water and teach the other children to swim."

"I think I will sit a little while longer," said the mother. "I have sat so long, a day or two more won't matter."

"Very well, please yourself," said the old duck, rising; and she went away.

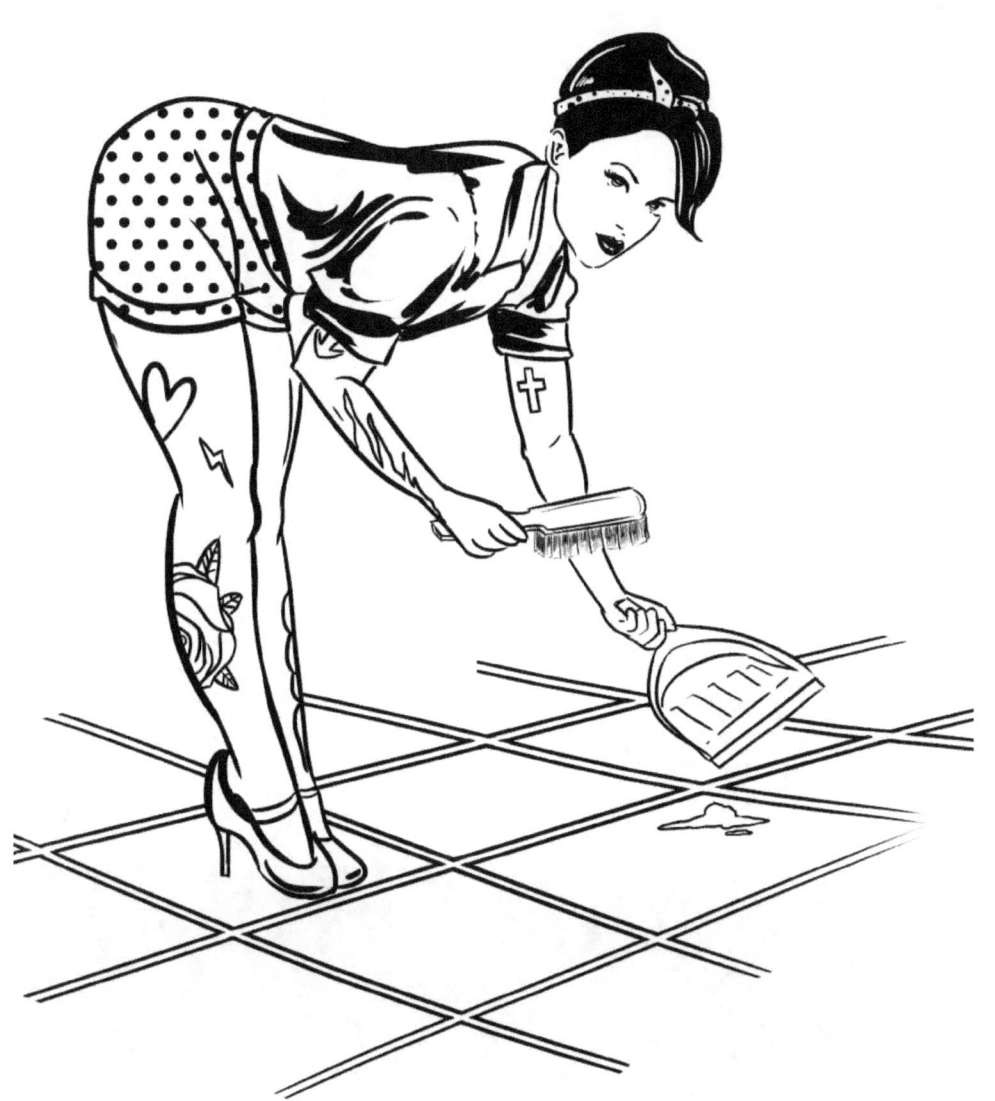

Chicken Scratch

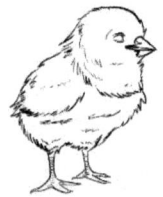

At last the great egg broke, and the latest bird cried "Peep, peep," as he crept forth from the shell. How big and ugly he was! The mother duck stared at him and did not know what to think. "Really," she said, "this is an enormous duckling, and it is not at all like any of the others. I wonder if he will turn out to be a Guinea fowl. Well, we shall see when we get to the water—for into the water he must go, even if I have to push him in myself."

On the next day the weather was delightful. The sun shone brightly on the green burdock leaves, and the mother duck took her whole family down to the water and jumped in with a splash. "Quack, quack!" cried she, and one after another the little ducklings jumped in. The water closed over their heads, but they came up again in an instant and swam about quite prettily, with their legs paddling under them as easily as possible; their legs went of their own accord; and the ugly gray-coat was also in the water, swimming with them.

"Oh," said the mother, "that is not a Guinea fowl. See how well he uses his legs, and how erect he holds himself! He is my own child, and he is not so very ugly after all, if you look at him properly. Quack, quack! come with me now. I will take you into grand society and introduce you to the farmyard, but you must keep close to me or you may be trodden upon; and, above all, beware of the cat."

When they reached the farmyard, there was a wretched riot going on; two families were fighting for an eel's head, which, after all, was carried off by the cat. "See, children, that is the way of the world," said the mother duck, whetting her beak, for she would have liked the eel's head herself. "Come, now, use your legs, and let me see how well you can behave. You must bow your heads prettily to that old duck yonder; she is the highest born of them all and has Spanish blood; therefore she is well off. Don't you see she has a red rag tied to her leg, which is something very grand and a great honor for a duck; it shows that everyone is anxious not to lose her, and that she is to be noticed by both man and beast. Come, now, don't turn in your toes; a well-bred duckling spreads

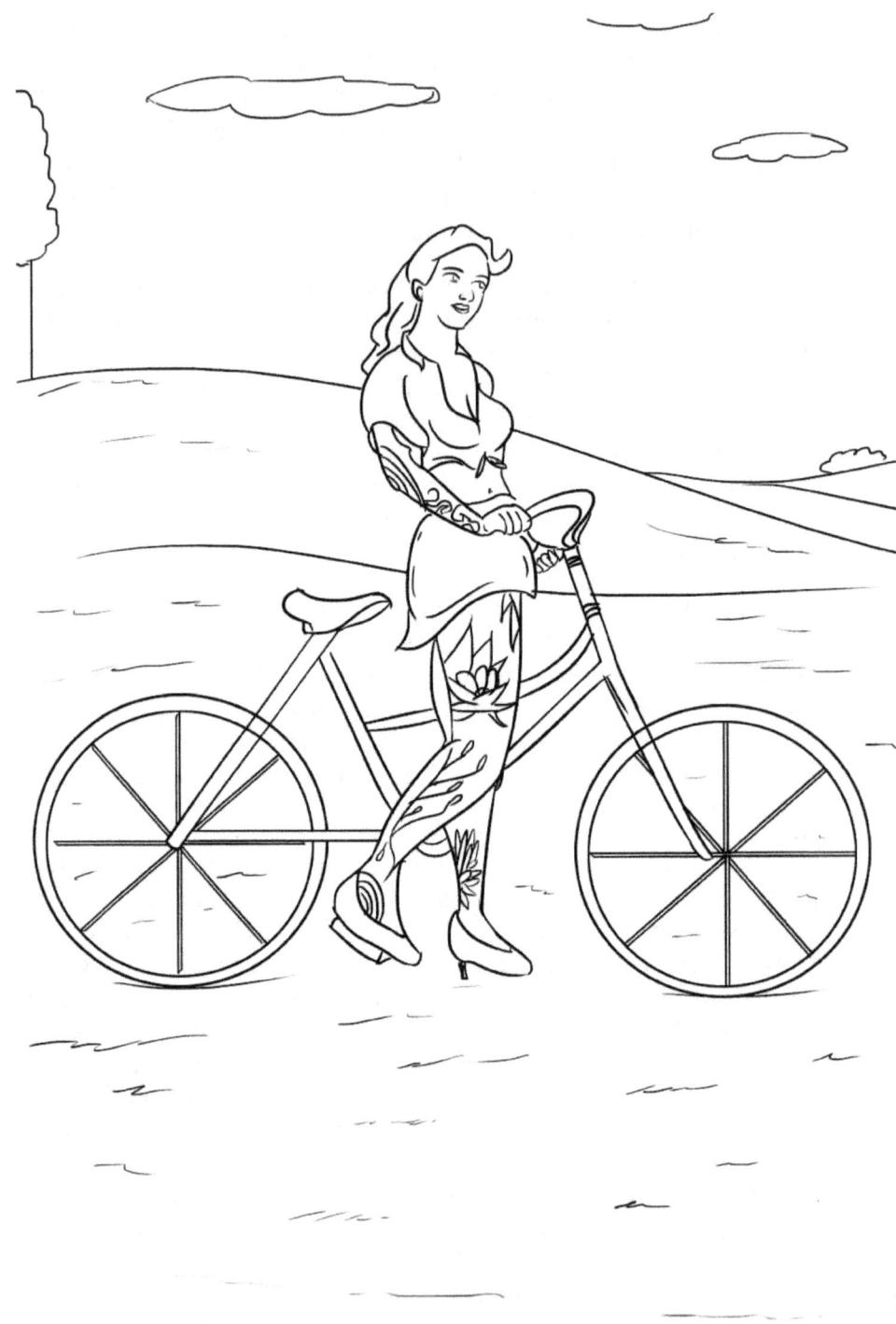

Chicken Scratch

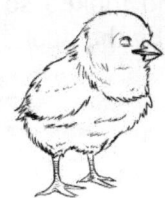

his feet wide apart, just like his father and mother, in this way; now bend your necks and say 'Quack!

The ducklings did as they were bade, but the other ducks stared, and said, "Look, here comes another brood—as if there were not enough of us already! And bless me, what a queer-looking object one of them is; we don't want him here"; and then one flew out and bit him in the neck.

"Let him alone," said the mother; "he is not doing any harm."

"Yes, but he is so big and ugly. He's a perfect fright," said the spiteful duck, "and therefore he must be turned out. A little biting will do him good."

"The others are very pretty children," said the old duck with the rag on her leg, "all but that one. I wish his mother could smooth him up a bit; he is really ill-favored."

"That is impossible, your grace," replied the mother. "He is not pretty, but he has a very good disposition and swims as well as the others or even better. I think he will grow up pretty, and perhaps be smaller. He has remained too long in the egg, and therefore his figure is not properly formed;" and then she stroked his neck and smoothed the feathers, saying: "It is a drake, and therefore not of so much consequence. I think he will grow up strong and able to take care of himself."

"The other ducklings are graceful enough," said the old duck. "Now make yourself at home, and if you find an eel's head you can bring it to me."

And so they made themselves comfortable; but the poor duckling who had crept out of his shell last of all and looked so ugly was bitten and pushed and made fun of, not only by the ducks but by all the poultry.

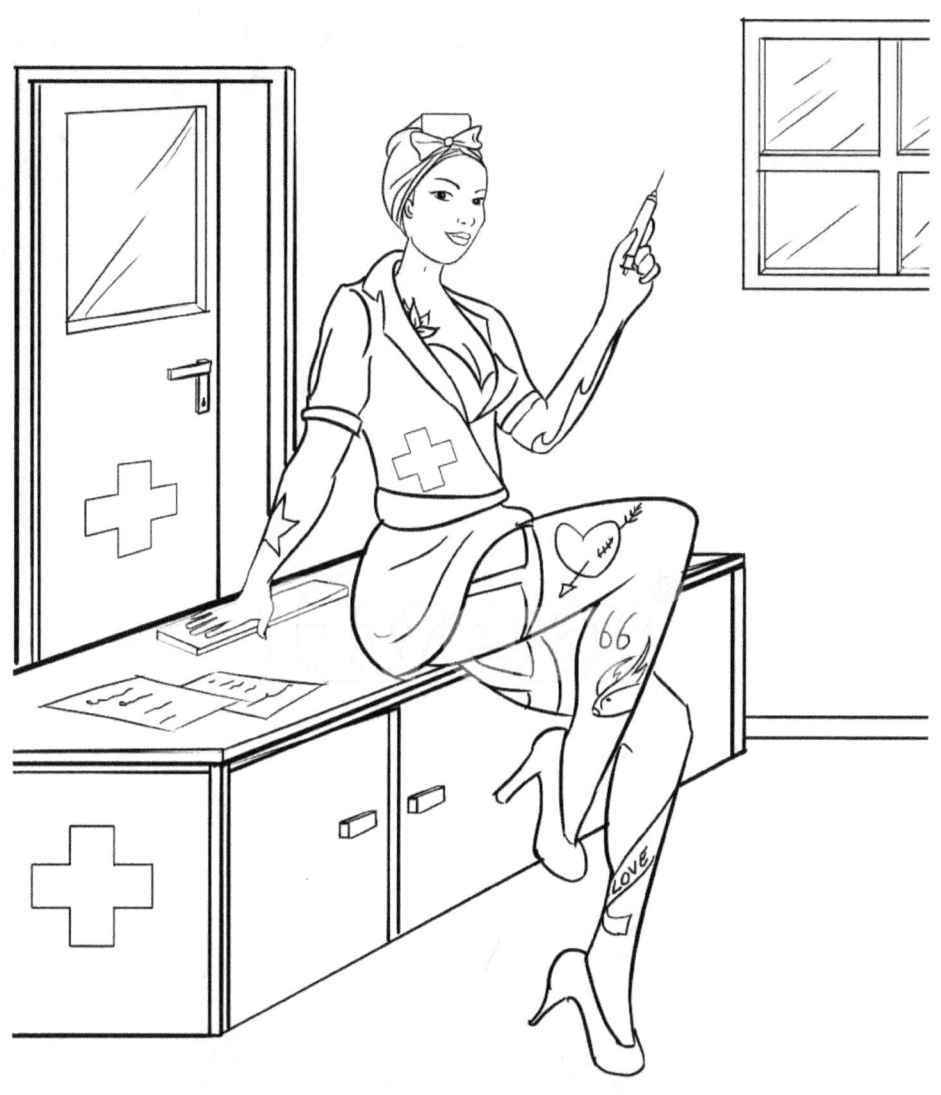

Chicken Scratch

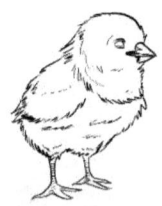

"He is too big," they all said; and the turkey cock, who had been born into the world with spurs and fancied himself really an emperor, puffed himself out like a vessel in full sail and flew at the duckling. He became quite red in the head with passion, so that the poor little thing did not know where to go, and was quite miserable because he was so ugly as to be laughed at by the whole farmyard.

So it went on from day to day; it got worse and worse. The poor duckling was driven about by every one; even his brothers and sisters were unkind to him and would say, "Ah, you ugly creature, I wish the cat would get you" and his mother had been heard to say she wished he had never been born. The ducks pecked him, the chickens beat him, and the girl who fed the poultry pushed him with her feet. So at last he ran away, frightening the little birds in the hedge as he flew over the palings. "They are afraid because I am so ugly," he said. So he flew still farther, until he came out on a large moor inhabited by wild ducks. Here he remained the whole night, feeling very sorrowful.

In the morning, when the wild ducks rose in the air, they stared at their new comrade. "What sort of a duck are you?" they all said, coming round him.

He bowed to them and was as polite as he could be, but he did not reply to their question. "You are exceedingly ugly," said the wild ducks; "but that will not matter if you do not want to marry one of our family."

Poor thing! he had no thoughts of marriage; all he wanted was permission to lie among the rushes and drink some of the water on the moor. After he had been on the moor two days, there came two wild geese, or rather goslings, for they had not been out of the egg long, which accounts for their impertinence. "Listen, friend," said one of them to the duckling; "you are so ugly that we like you very well. Will you go with us and become a bird of passage? Not far from here is another moor, in which there are some wild geese, all of them unmarried. It is a chance for you to get a wife. You may make your fortune, ugly as you are."

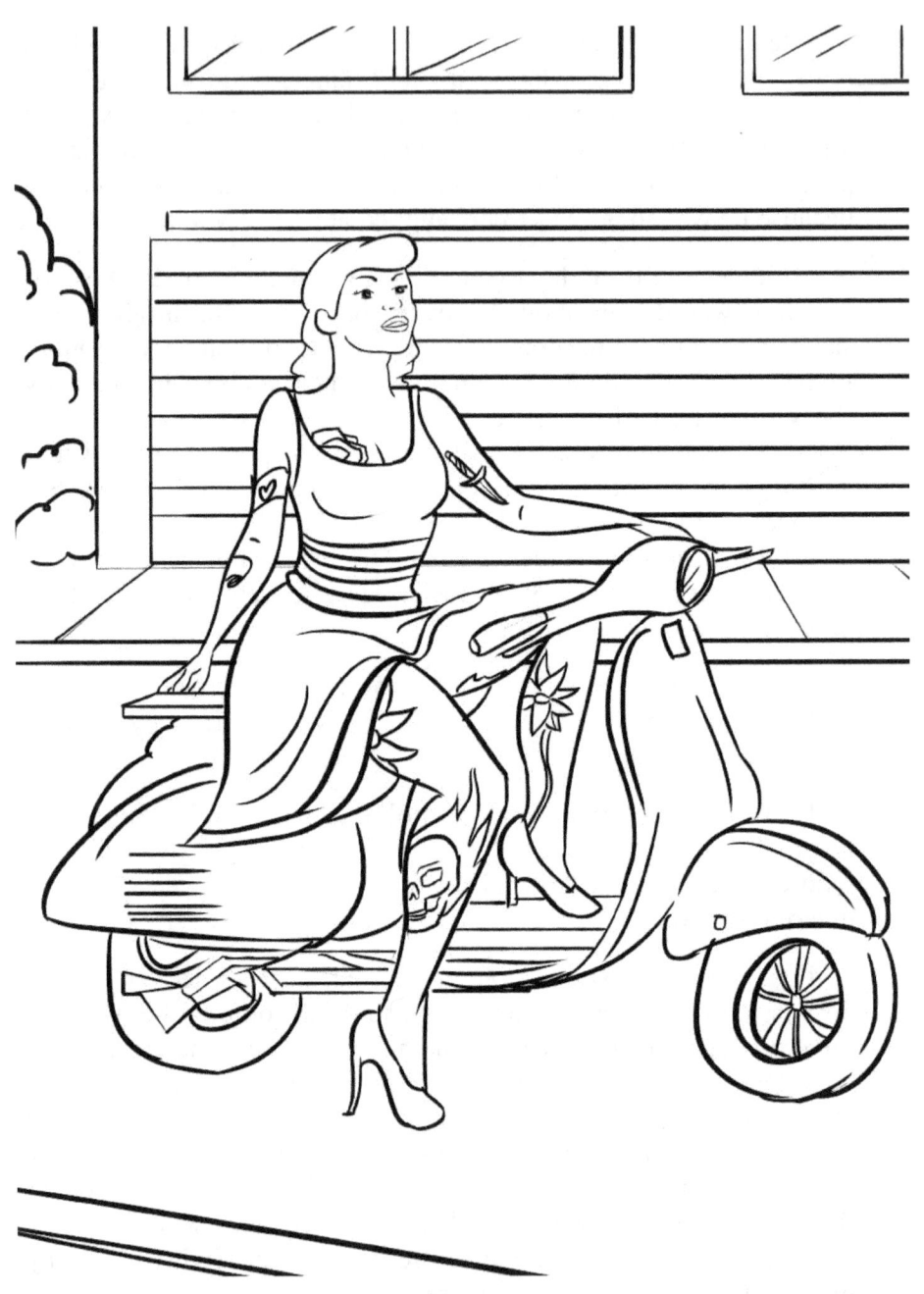

Chicken Scratch

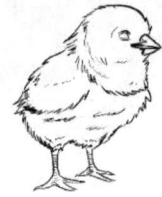

"Bang, bang," sounded in the air, and the two wild geese fell dead among the rushes, and the water was tinged with blood.

"Bang, bang," echoed far and wide in the distance, and whole flocks of wild geese rose up from the rushes.

The sound continued from every direction, for the sportsmen surrounded the moor, and some were even seated on branches of trees, overlooking the rushes. The blue smoke from the guns rose like clouds over the dark trees, and as it floated away across the water, a number of sporting dogs bounded in among the rushes, which bent beneath them wherever they went. How they terrified the poor duckling! He turned away his head to hide it under his wing, and at the same moment a large, terrible dog passed quite near him. His jaws were open, his tongue hung from his mouth, and his eyes glared fearfully. He thrust his nose close to the duckling, showing his sharp teeth, and then "splash, splash," he went into the water, without touching him.

"Oh," sighed the duckling, "how thankful I am for being so ugly; even a dog will not bite me." And so he lay quite still, while the shot rattled through the rushes, and gun after gun was fired over him. It was late in the day before all became quiet, but even then the poor young thing did not dare to move. He waited quietly for several hours and then, after looking carefully around him, hastened away from the moor as fast as he could. He ran over field and meadow till a storm arose, and he could hardly struggle against it.

Towards evening he reached a poor little cottage that seemed ready to fall, and only seemed to remain standing because it could not decide on which side to fall first. The storm continued so violent that the duckling could go no farther. He sat down by the cottage, and then he noticed that the door was not quite closed, in consequence of one of the hinges having given way.

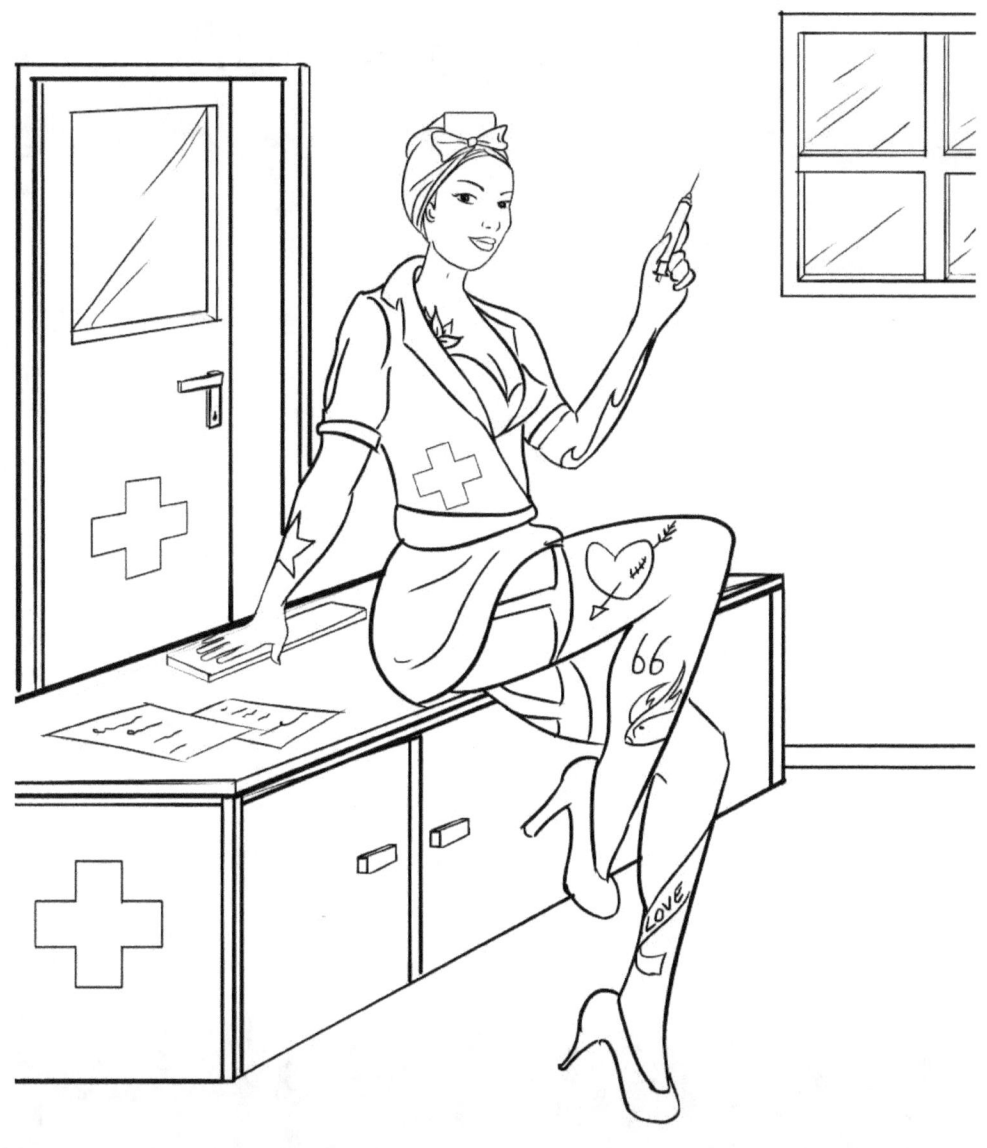

Chicken Scratch

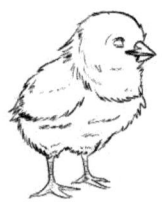

There was, therefore, a narrow opening near the bottom large enough for him to slip through, which he did very quietly, and got a shelter for the night. Here, in this cottage, lived a woman, a cat, and a hen. The cat, whom his mistress called "My little son," was a great favorite; he could raise his back, and purr, and could even throw out sparks from his fur if it were stroked the wrong way.

The hen had very short legs, so she was called "Chickie Short-legs." She laid good eggs, and her mistress loved her as if she had been her own child. In the morning the strange visitor was discovered; the cat began to purr and the hen to cluck.

"What is that noise about?" said the old woman, looking around the room. But her sight was not very good; therefore when she saw the duckling she thought it must be a fat duck that had strayed from home. "Oh, what a prize!" she exclaimed. "I hope it is not a drake, for then I shall have some ducks' eggs. I must wait and see."

So the duckling was allowed to remain on trial for three weeks; but there were no eggs.

Now the cat was the master of the house, and the hen was the mistress; and they always said, "We and the world," for they believed themselves to be half the world, and by far the better half, too. The duckling thought that others might hold a different opinion on the subject, but the hen would not listen to such doubts.

"Can you lay eggs?" she asked. "No." "Then have the goodness to cease talking." "Can you raise your back, or purr, or throw out sparks?" said the cat. "No." "Then you have no right to express an opinion when sensible people are speaking." So the duckling sat in a corner, feeling very low-spirited; but when the sunshine and the fresh air came into the room through the open door, he began to feel such a great longing for a swim that he could not help speaking of it.

"What an absurd idea!" said the hen. "You have nothing else to do; therefore you have foolish fancies. If you could purr or lay eggs, they would pass away."

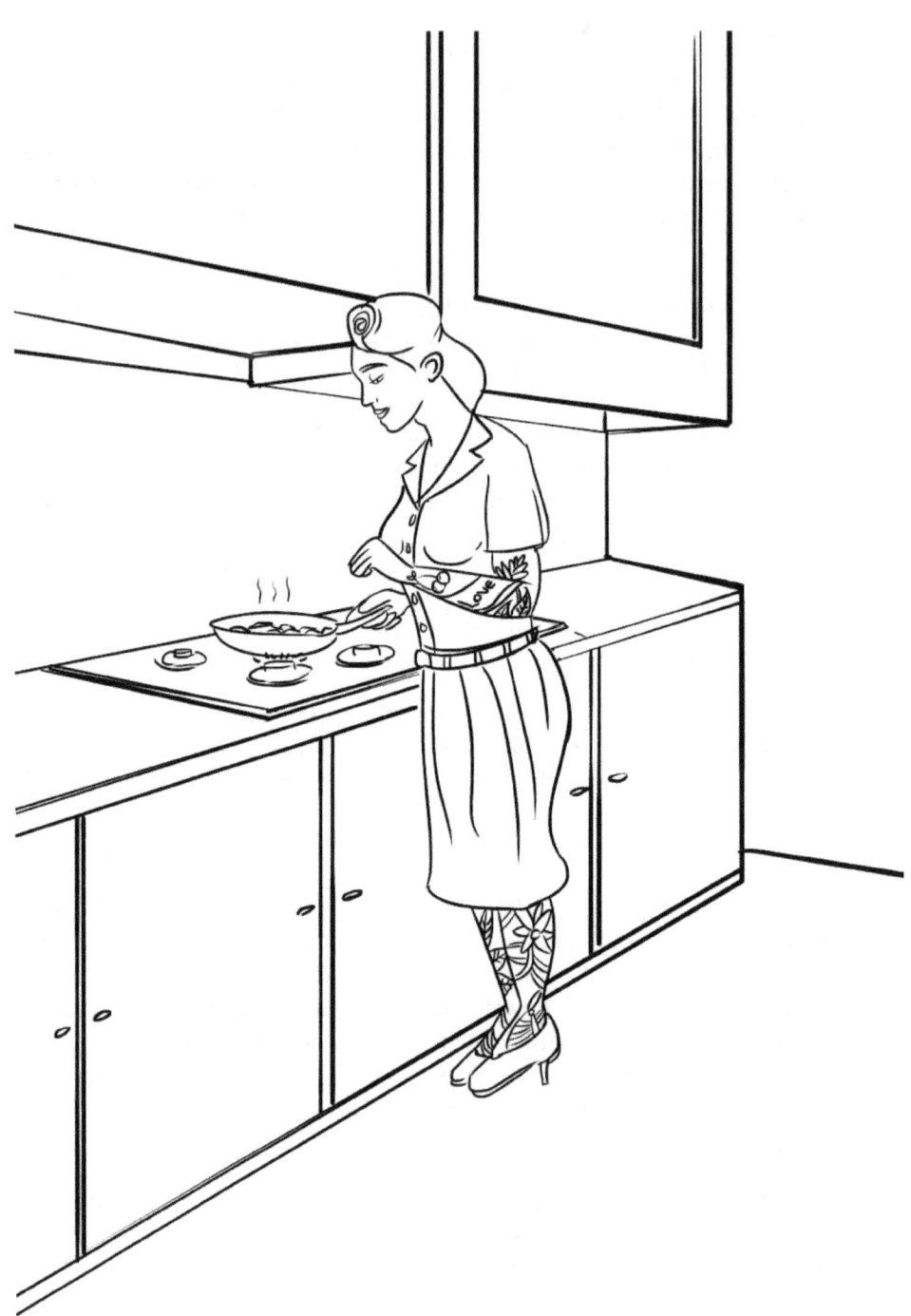

Chicken Scratch

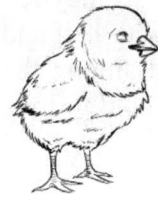

"But it is so delightful to swim about on the water," said the duckling, "and so refreshing to feel it close over your head while you dive down to the bottom."

"Delightful, indeed! it must be a queer sort of pleasure," said the hen. "Why, you must be crazy! Ask the cat—he is the cleverest animal I know; ask him how he would like to swim about on the Insert chapter one text here.

` water, or to dive under it, for I will not speak of my own opinion. Ask our mistress, the old woman; there is no one in the world more clever than she is. Do you think she would relish swimming and letting the water close over her head?"

"I see you don't understand me," said the duckling.

"We don't understand you? Who can understand you, I wonder? Do you consider yourself more clever than the cat or the old woman?—I will say nothing of myself. Don't imagine such nonsense, child, and thank your good fortune that you have been so well received here. Are you not in a warm room and in society from which you may learn something? But you are a chatterer, and your company is not very agreeable. Believe me, I speak only for your good. I may tell you unpleasant truths, but that is a proof of my friendship. I advise you, therefore, to lay eggs and learn to purr as quickly as possible."

"I believe I must go out into the world again," said the duckling.

"Yes, do," said the hen. So the duckling left the cottage and soon found water on which it could swim and dive, but he was avoided by all other animals because of his ugly appearance.

Autumn came, and the leaves in the forest turned to orange and gold; then, as winter approached, the wind caught them as they fell and whirled them into the cold air. The clouds, heavy with hail and snowflakes, hung low in the sky, and the raven stood among the reeds, crying, "Croak, croak." It made one shiver with cold to look at him. All this was very sad for the poor little duckling.

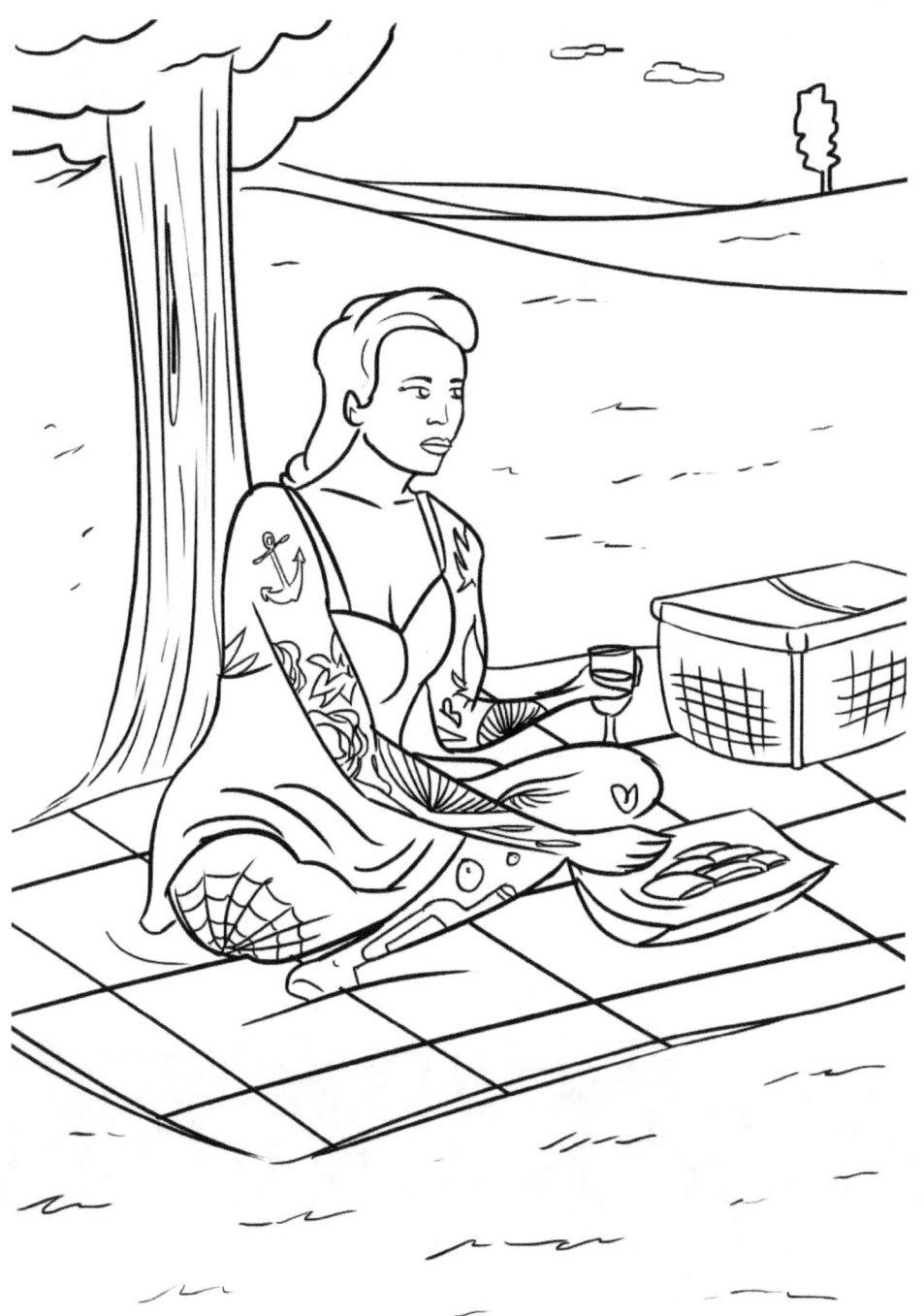

Chicken Scratch

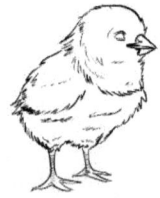

One evening, just as the sun was setting amid radiant clouds, there came a large flock of beautiful birds out of the bushes. The duckling had never seen any like them before. They were swans; and they curved their graceful necks, while their soft plumage shone with dazzling whiteness. They uttered a singular cry as they spread their glorious wings and flew away from those cold regions to warmer countries across the sea. They mounted higher and higher in the air, and the ugly little duckling had a strange sensation as he watched them. He whirled himself in the water like a wheel, stretched out his neck towards them, and uttered a cry

so strange that it frightened even himself. Could he ever forget those beautiful, happy birds! And when at last they were out of his sight, he dived under the water and rose again almost beside himself with excitement. He knew not the names of these birds nor where they had flown, but he felt towards them as he had never felt towards any other bird in the world. He was not envious of these beautiful creatures; it never occurred to him to wish to be as lovely as they. Poor ugly creature, how gladly he would have lived even with the ducks, had they only treated him kindly and given him encouragement.

The winter grew colder and colder; he was obliged to swim about on the water to keep it from freezing, but every night the space on which he swam became smaller and smaller. At length it froze so hard that the ice in the water

and carried the duckling home to his wife. The warmth revived the poor little creature; but when the children wanted to play with him, the duckling thought they would do him some harm, so he started up in terror, fluttered into the milk pan, and splashed the milk about the room. Then the woman clapped her hands, which frightened him still more. He flew first into the butter cask, then into the meal tub and out again. What a condition he was in! The woman screamed and struck at him with the tongs; the children laughed and screamed and tumbled over each other in their efforts to catch him, but luckily he escaped. The door stood open; the poor creature could just manage to slip out among the bushes and lie down quite exhausted in the newly fallen snow.

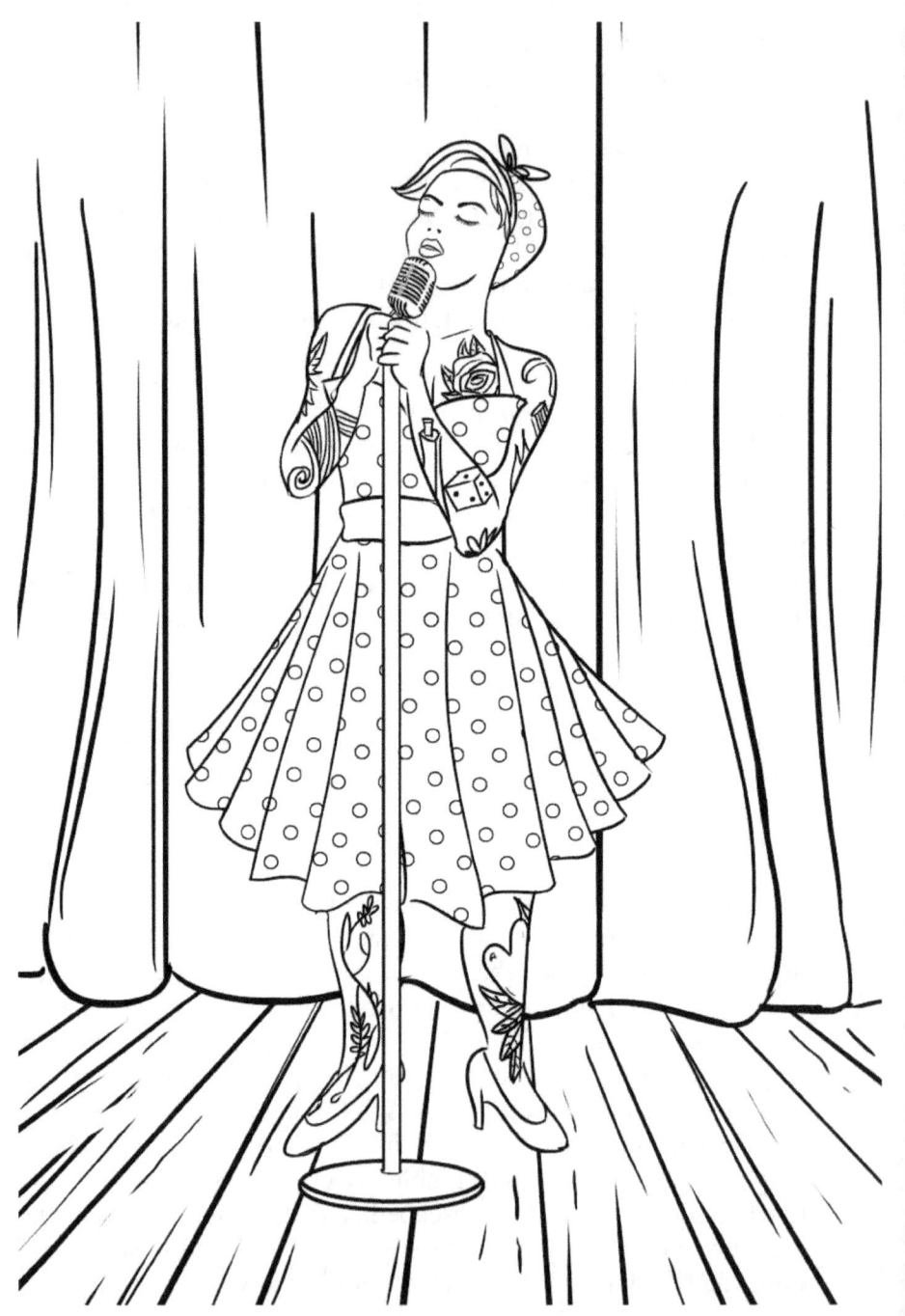

Chicken Scratch

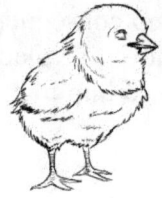

It would be very sad were I to relate all the misery and privations which the poor little duckling endured during the hard winter; but when it had passed he found himself lying one morning in a moor, amongst the rushes. He felt the warm sun shining and heard the lark singing and saw that all around was beautiful spring.

Then the young bird felt that his wings were strong, as he flapped them against his sides and rose high into the air. They bore him onwards until, before he well knew how it had happened, he found himself in a large garden. The apple trees were in full blossom, and the fragrant elders bent their long green branches down to the stream, which wound round a smooth lawn. Everything looked beautiful in the freshness of early spring. From a thicket close by came three beautiful white swans, rustling their feathers and swimming lightly over the smooth water. The duckling saw these lovely birds and felt more strangely unhappy than ever.

"I will fly to these royal birds," he exclaimed, "and they will kill me because, ugly as I am, I dare to approach them. But it does not matter; better be killed by them than pecked by the ducks, beaten by the hens, pushed about by the maiden who feeds the poultry, or starved with hunger in the winter."

Then he flew to the water and swam towards the beautiful swans. The moment they espied the stranger they rushed to meet him with outstretched wings.

"Kill me," said the poor bird and he bent his head down to the surface of the water and awaited death.

But what did he see in the clear stream below? His own image—no longer a dark-gray bird, ugly and disagreeable to look at, but a graceful and beautiful swan.

To be born in a duck's nest in a farmyard is of no consequence to a bird if it is hatched from a swan's egg. He now felt glad at having suffered sorrow and trouble, because it enabled him to

Chicken Scratch

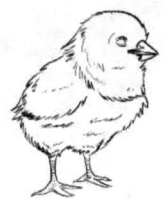

enjoy so much better all the pleasure and happiness around him; for the great swans swam round the newcomer and stroked his neck with their beaks, as a welcome.

Into the garden presently came some little children and threw bread and cake into the water.

"See," cried the youngest, "there is a new one;" and the rest were delighted, and ran to their father and mother, dancing and clapping their hands and shouting joyously, "There is another swan come; a new one has arrived."

Then they threw more bread and cake into the water and said, "The new one is the most beautiful of all, he is so young and pretty." And the old swans bowed their heads before him.

Then he felt quite ashamed and hid his head under his wing, for he did not know what to do, he was so happy—yet he was not at all proud. He had been persecuted and despised for his ugliness, and now he heard them say he was the most beautiful of all the birds. Even the elder tree bent down its boughs into the water before him, and the sun shone warm and bright. Then he rustled his feathers, curved his slender neck, and cried joyfully, from the depths of his heart, "I never dreamed of such happiness as this while I was the despised ugly duckling."

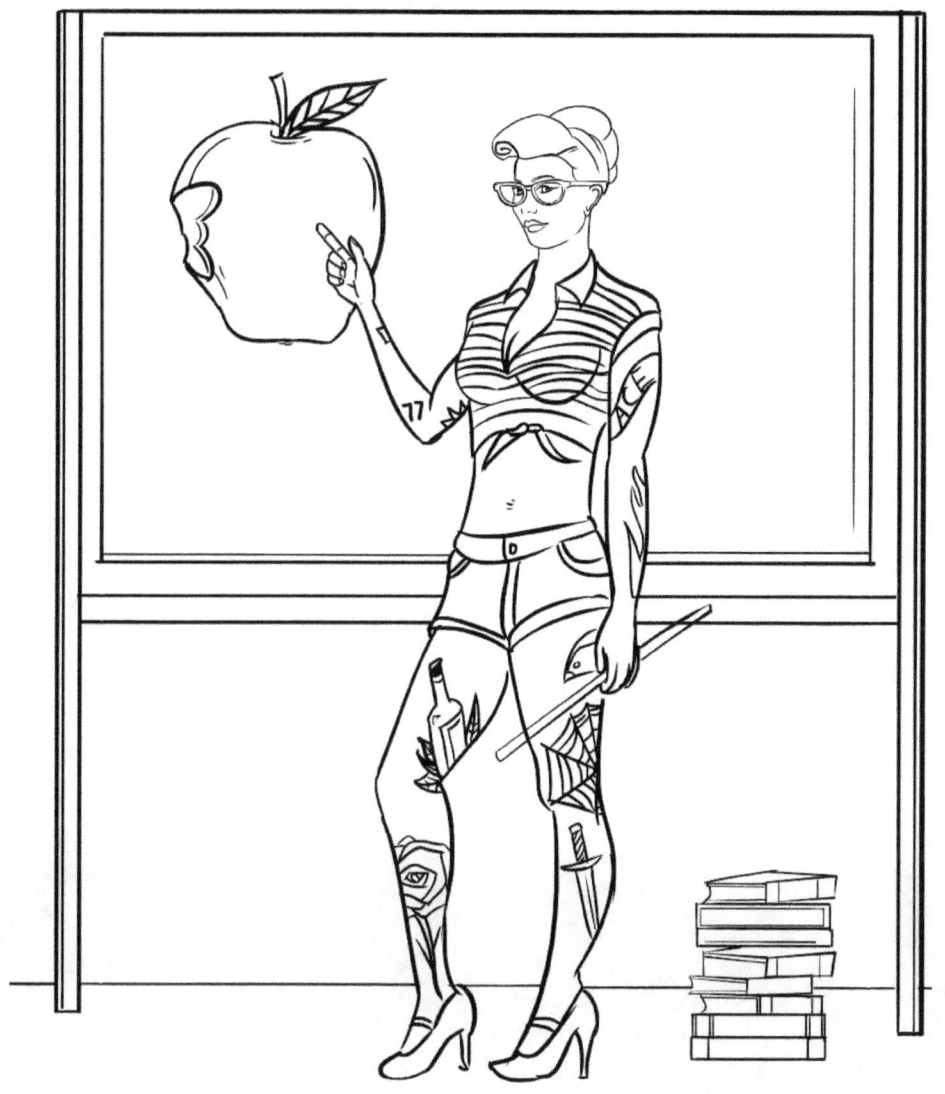

Chicken Scratch

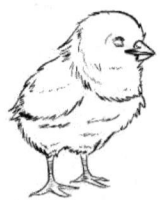

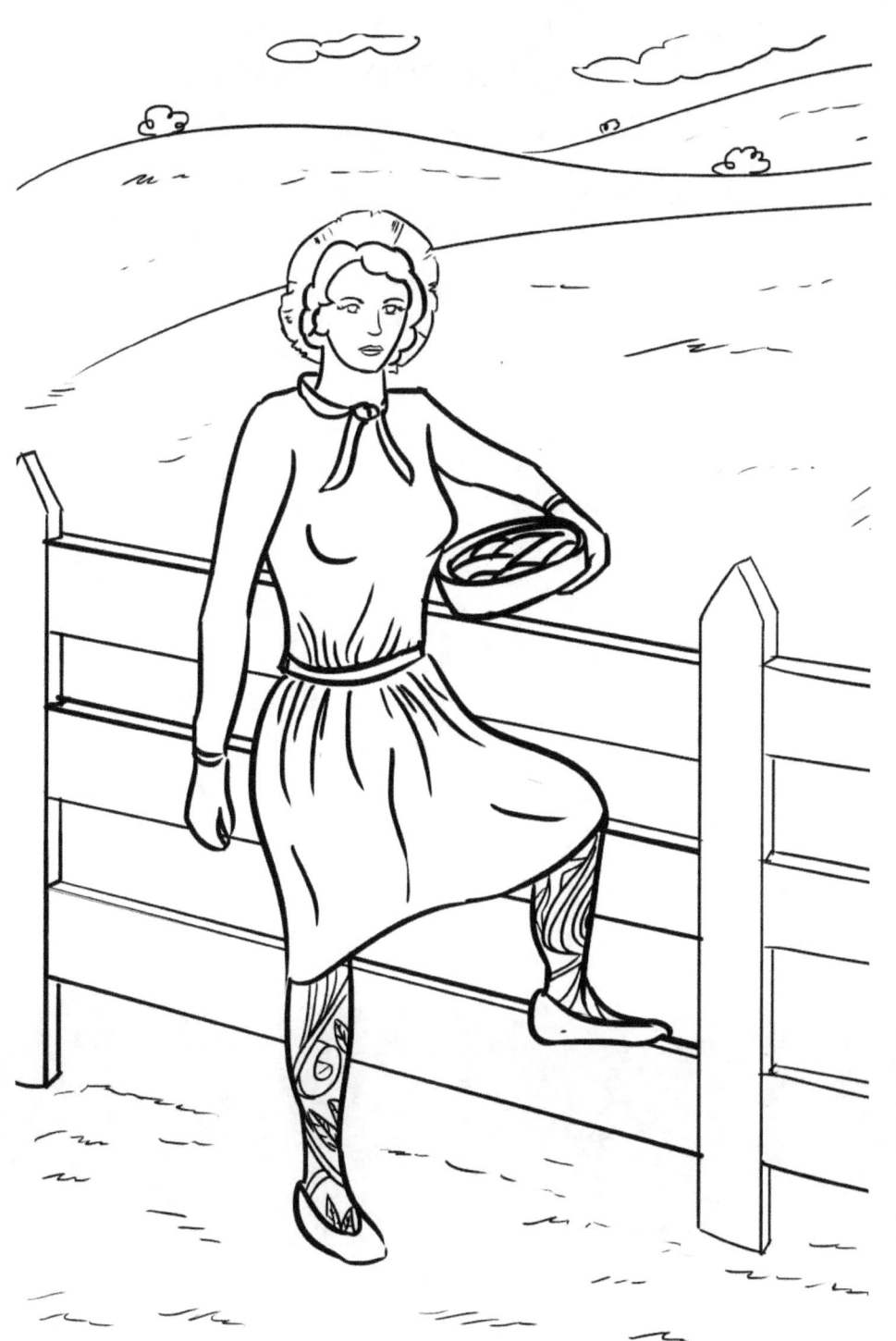

Chicken Scratch

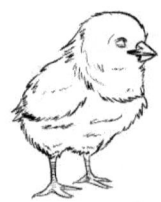

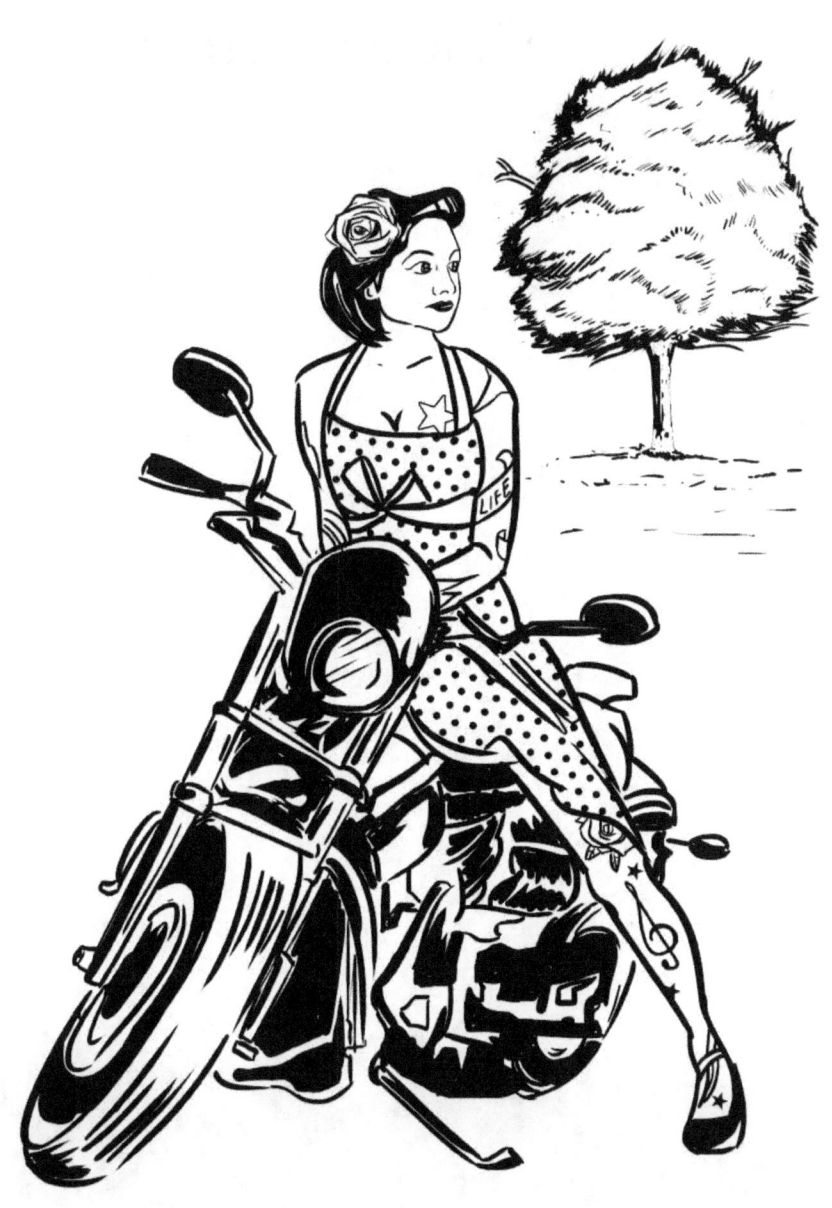

Chicken Scratch

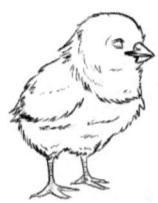

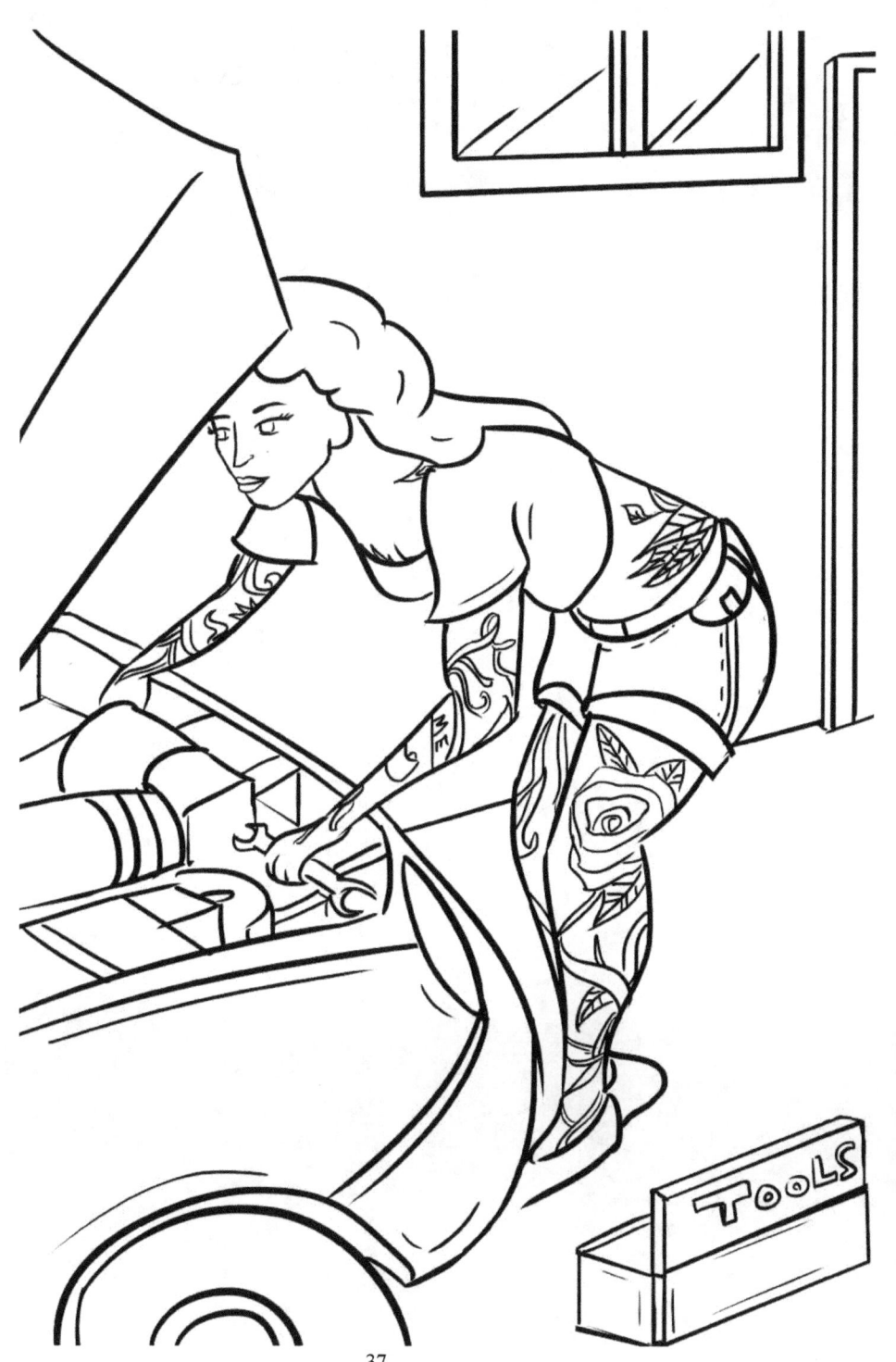

Chicken Scratch

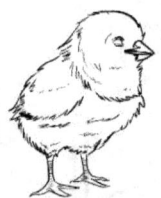

Chicken Scratch

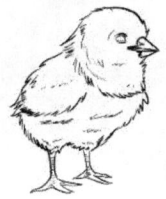

Chicken Scratch

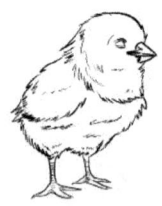